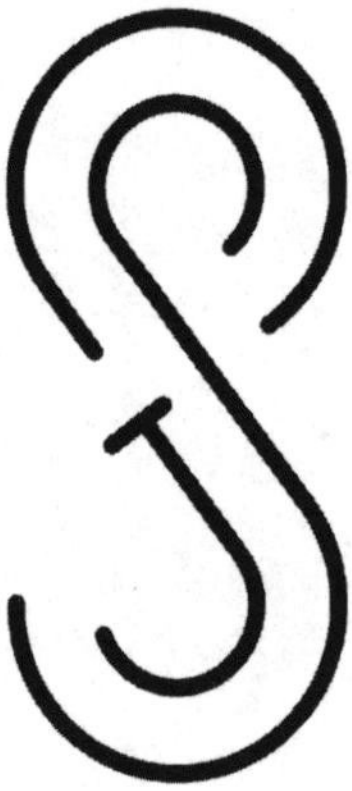

*Brian,*

*You must create*

Stephen James Smith

*SjS*

# FEAR NOT

*26/9/18*

ARLEN
HOUSE

*Fear Not*

is published in 2018 by
ARLEN HOUSE
42 Grange Abbey Road
Baldoyle
Dublin 13
Ireland
Phone: 353 86 8360236
Email: arlenhouse@gmail.com
arlenhouse.blogspot.com


Distributed internationally by
SYRACUSE UNIVERSITY PRESS
621 Skytop Road, Suite 110
Syracuse, NY 13244–5290
Phone: 315–443–5534/Fax: 315–443–5545
Email: supress@syr.edu


978–1–85132–144–5, paperback

Typesetting by Arlen House

Cover images by Steve Simpson
are reproduced courtesy of the artist
www.stevesimpson.com

# CONTENTS

*us people, we're just poems*
– Ani DiFranco

Half 'n' half, curry chips
glass half full with snake bite bits
vomit, taxi, ATM ...

# FEAR NOT

TOOLING UP
*for the staff of IADT*

Thumbs down,
butchered,
guts in hand.
Thrown from the arena.

Now, I re-enter,
testing my fear,
steadying my hand,
striking forth.

If not for the ghosts,
my answers would be simple.
Now my questions
are sharpening my words.

My path back
has seen me become:
a barman, a salesman,
a chancer, a doormat.

Now, I'm methodically
disemboweling: authors, poets, theorists.
Hammering the fiery metal,
stoking alloyed arguments.

No Colosseum for me now.
The heat of the furnace
burns my brow, ignites my lungs,
and has made me a sword.

## Dublin You Are

_Commissioned by Dublin City Council for the 2020 European Capital_
_of Culture campaign_
_for Dr Kevin Wallace_
_in memory of Conor O'Riordan_

Dublin you are grey brick upon brick,
full of tarmac and hipster pricks?
Just face it, all other places Pale in comparison,
you are more than some former Saxon garrison.
Dublin your warmth came too late for John Corrie.
Dublin are you even sorry?
Dublin you are divided by more than the Liffey,
You said YES to equality
and it's about Blooming time.
Yet Dublin you always Proclaimed to cherish all!
Dublin your Panties are on Capel Street
compromising any Papal feats.
Dublin Jedward, awkward ...
Dublin you are more than a settlement on the Poddle,
But Dublin what's the craic with coddle?
It's shite, why don't we just admit it!
Dublin you brought back Sam again, but
Dublin when did you go from,
the clash of the ash, to exchanging gold for cash?
Dublin, Dyflin, Eblana, Baile Átha Cliath,
and 180 other tongues your citizens are using to name ya ...
So _céad míle fáilte_ to all.
Dublin where power is held by too few in the Dáil.
Dublin when will you revolt again?
1988 wasn't your true millennium
despite the 50ps and milk bottles.
Dublin you're mine, but I'm happy to share you.
Dublin from RTÉ, TCD, UCD, U2, SIPTU, IFSC
and acrimonious Temple Bar STDs, ODs and OMGs!
No longer the second city, yet you play second fiddle
to Google and Guinness,

to Facebook and unsociable twits.
Dublin look at yourself.

Dublin your tower blocks and tenements
are an excuse for a solution.
Dublin c'mere 'till I tell ya
you can be more than
rapid dirtbirds and banjaxed bowsies,
alrigh' story bud and yeah sure it's all good,
jaysis that's scaldy,
Why Go Baldy,
I'm excira and delira,
Dublin I cry for ya!
Dublin you're a tough bastard,
yet full of the softness of all of the people on your streets.
Margaret Dunne dancing on O'Connell Street,
The Diceman Tom McGinty miming on Grafton Street,
Pat Ingoldsby with his poems on Westmoreland Street,
and your Mollys: Malone, Ivers and Bloom.
To Daily-Sally-Sandy-Mounts ...
From the gospel of Kelly, Drew, McKenna and Sheahan,
to Borstal Boys like Brendan Behan.
Two Gallants reJoycing, and Eveline looking out to sea.
Snow falling slowly on *The Dead* in Glasnevin,
Glen and Markéta *Once* strolling,
to Christy Brown willfully controlling a foot
to paint pictures and poems.
To your heroines
Brenda Fricker the city's mother,
Maureen O'Hara an enchanting other.
Dublin you are boom and bust,
running Wilde and Swift.
Dublin can I trust you?
Dublin your true blue is Harry Clarke's cobalt.
Dublin from a Thin Lizzy, Dicey Reilly,

to a floozy in a jacuzzi God fearin'.
Dublin shooting down Veronica Guerin.

Dublin you are Bang-Bang, Fortycoats,
Zozimus a blind street poet.
Dublin you are all of us,
and all who are yet to come,
so let's go to the Gravediggers and have a pint.
Dublin remember Stardust and all your waltzing lovers.
Dublin Big Jim's arms are outstretched to a *Risen People*,
yet are we under the thumb again?
Dublin your GPO columns are scarred from *The Crackle* of
    gunshots.
Dublin your CCTV will never yield your essence like the shots
of Arthur Fields' Man on Bridge.
You are the Poolbeg Towers,
and the poor shower
begging on Bachelor's Walk.
Dublin you're all talk, yet you have my attention,
from Robbie Keane to Paula Meehan.
Dublin's calling, *ohh ahh* Paul McGrath,
while some say 'Up the RA'.
Dublin bridging caps with Joyce and Beckett
and finally to Rosie Hackett!
Dublin Paddy Finnegan was forced to sell
*The Big Issue* on your streets,
while 'Daffodil Mulligan' was played to bodhrán beats.
Dublin you say delish,
Dublin you are full of Polish
and Brazilians speaking Portuguese,
and now the Chinese
have turned Parnell Street into Chinatown.
Dublin don't let them down.
Dublin don't forget *no blacks, no dogs, no Irish,*
Dublin perish the thought of you being racist.

Dublin Cú Chulainn has fled the GPO,
and heading for Monto.

Dublin your bay embraces despite the Sellafield Sea,
and your mountains frame all your natural beauty.
Dublin a wailing banshee stricken with TB,
Dublin you're European, but could be Craggy Island in
    disguise?
Gabriel Conroy is heading west because of an epiphany.
Just sayin' Dublin you only painted your post boxes green!
Is The Abbey doing all you'd dreamed?
Dublin you are Notorious for clampers, senators and seagulls,
to Celtic Tiger and septic tanks
to singing High Kings and rampaging Vikings.
Dublin cm'ere,
take me for a Teddy's and a romantic stroll down the pier ...
Dublin you are
a dancing place, a sprawling space
of villages and many faces on the edge
of an island that's eroded by the Atlantic,
battling with being romanticised.
Dublin are you dynamic?
Struggling with identity?
Changing for the better?
Changing for us?
Dublin don't be scared
to change.
Don't be
scared!
We're
with you.
Always.
Dublin.
My friend.
My home.

Mentioned
50 times
in this poem.

We live in you.
My city,
*mo chroí,*
I love you,
most of the time.
You see …
Dublin You Are
Me!

*Dublin Sun* (Matt Griffin)

My mother calls me,
says, 'please wherever you are
look at the sunset'.

*The Family* (Karen Hickey)

## THE GARDENER
*for Sandra*

She turned to me and said,
*do you think I am happy?*
And I heard a question
I didn't want to hear.

I knew the answer.
I have listened to the cry.
But to face it made me uneasy.
But I felt the bravery,
I felt the realness in the moment.

So I answered.

You see, she is a gardener
who has great plans,
but works with what she has got.
She loves creation, sees beauty
and wants to share it with you.

She sees the cruelty of nature
and understands its power.
Yet it fills her with wonder.

Have you tried her rhubarb
fresh from granny's garden?
You should!

Maybe there are prettier roses,
but she'd rather be a cooking apple.
Or better yet a gooseberry.

Her hands are worn,
the flesh loosened by age.

She held my hand in church today,
for the first time in too long.

Her eyes are still young,
still life to be lived.

This 'Jo Bangles' is not condemned,
when there is breath left.

Still seeking that happiness,
God love her!

'People before profit', she says,
a modern day Guevara or Connolly,
as a nation lets her down.
Working 34 years in a job
draining away her very essence.

For what?

To feed me,
educate me,
clothe me.

But not stopping there ...

I remember she took me
to Mrs Prendergast's near Butlins,
when we couldn't afford to go to Butlins.
Caravanning in Roundwood
with takeaway Chinese,
the Isle of Man, the theatre,
Tuesdays swimming,
cinema in Coolock on Saturday,

where I got most of the popcorn,
jazz after church every Sunday,
as we did today 28 years on.

Taught me to notice the sunset.

Her bondage, a sick child
and broken marriage.
All this, and I don't know
how to speak to her.
I always want to hug her,
and don't know how.

So a veiled kiss laced in courtesy will do.

She has been learning,
how to stop living
inside her own head.
Gets up, goes out.
Half the battle.

No panic attacks for a while.

Still manic,
but calmer now.
Still pretending.
Still xenophobic,
homophobic.
Not meaning to be.

Lost marbles down gutters like dreams.

The anger is fresher though,
built up over years

of false dawns, and mistrust.
Reduced expectations, frustrations.

Wants contentment now.

Quiet.
Yes, quiet.
Peace.

Or, perhaps
bird song
in her garden
where she will grow
rhubarb, strawberries,
apples, pears,
spuds, raspberries
and gooseberries.

Watch them bloom again,

and return to the soil,
but not before
she has lived a life deserving.

My mother told me today,
she pretends to be happy.
What do you say to that?
Let's watch her flower now I say,

and bring her some water.

## ON THE BUS
*for Ben*

I was on the bus and
this sunset it screamed
at me, reminding me of life,
reminding me to shine. And
I wanted to tell someone
to look at it and gaze at it
with me. But I paused and
the view, it had passed,
confiscated by concrete,
stolen by gravity. So
I phoned a friend on
a 50/50 chance that they
would see my end
and I sent my friend
a picture of it verbally.
'It was like a neon sign',
I said. No, that is shit. It
was like someone had
gotten all the flamingos and
pureed them, and concrete
clouds, dark and dull, had
puke-pulped guts glazed
on their undersides and
drips that drop into my
eyes. I speak no lies. But
the centre, the core, it was
like fire. Yes, ok, I know that
the sun is fire, but it was really
like fire that was friendly
and kind to touch. And
that sunset it touched me. So
let it touch you
and accept love

and accept that
things they are
intended to
be given like
beauty or a
heart or life
but accept
love!

*The Gardener* (Annemarie Menzies)

## BIRD-CAGED

I

She rings me,
(who's she, the cat's mother?)
to tell me there's a beautiful sunset
and that I should write a poem about it.

But I only get the voicemail,
the echo effect.
I call back, seeking
murmurs, embers.

'Look now to the east', I'm told.
'The colours! The colours!
Purples, blues, pinks.
Magic! Just magic!'

I cannot tell her
it does not
work like that.
I cannot tell her.

II

And in her voice,
I hear of another time.
Her fluttering in
the living room, bird-like.

'Can you see them, the little birds,
little bluebirds, as they go, in and out of the box.
Can you see?' She has binoculars to bolster
the sight of her hawk eyes. She spies.

It's not that I don't care
about what she is saying. I do.
I can feel the life of her, but all I hear
is her favourite Tchaikovsky piano concerto

as she moves with its rhythm
full of unexpected pauses, syncopations,
the changing for longer notes and on
to a gradual and expected crescendo.

But oh no!
'I can't let him die in the garden!' she says,
'I have to give him a chance!'
The bluebirds have left the nest.

Like me.
No
one
behind.

She picks the chick up
in her hands.

All petted plumage
in her hands,

tries,
helps
it fly.
Featherlike.

Demonstrating, while
recounting the tale,
the panic of life
to me.

After gravity.
Earthbound.
She hovered.
Hoovered

out the bird-box,
fresh for new nests.
And bird down
now.

Those days, though,
have flown. I return home
when she is away
to clean the cage.

To let Sukey,
her pet cockatiel, fly,
to take off again for
a while.

Sukey squawks, talks,
tells the lines to me,
that the bird brain's
been taught:

'Don't worry,
be happy'.
'Give us a kiss'.
'13 Ashton Grove' (our old unlucky home).

Till they've all gone away
after I've Hoovered
out a box of bird shite.
I trap wings again

for there's
no sunset here
and this poem's
flown.

YOUR HAND
*for Kata*

Do you remember how
I just kissed your hand?
Do you? Do you remember that?

I'm somewhat surprised by my reaction.
I've been caught in confusion, distraction
now at this delusional state, so we face our fate.

Do you remember Merrion Square?
There were many things there
that day and then, then there was us.

Do you remember when
I took photos of your feet?
And they were in the grass

and the light did something new.
Do you remember that?
Do you?

We're saying goodbye now.
But I sing you that song
*We'll meet again, don't know where, don't know when ...*

And I whisper you that poem, the one called
'On the Bus'. What was it I said about accepting love?
Do you remember? Do you?

I bought you some books, but I never
wrote a message inside. I couldn't, well I could,
but I don't know why I couldn't.

Sure shouldn't
these things
just come to you?

Do you remember the flowers?
I saw lots of flowers with you,
I did.

And what about the time we met,
that was great, wasn't it?
There was something there.

Yeah,
there was something there
alright!

But do you remember how
I kissed your hand?
Do you remember that?

I just kissed your hand …
And the way we just hugged,
it meant something to me.

Yeah,
it meant something
alright.

And I,
I wasn't
going

to cry
well I wasn't
until you did.

## DEAD MAN'S SHIRT
*for Kate*

'My tongue will tell the anger of my heart
Or else my heart concealing it will break'
Katherina Minola, *The Taming of the Shrew*


Terry's cotton shirt is pressed on my back.
He passed last October,
this my memento of a dead man,
her uncle, whom I never met.

We joked that if we broke up
I'd have to give back his shirts, yet
we parted a month ago and here I am
in the London Irish Centre, still draped in him.

I wanted to have a Mulqueen's presence
again in this place, on these foreign shores,
a little piece of Limerick in London,
the diaspora returned so to speak.

Bringing together tributaries contributing
from the Shannon and Thames with names
of all the other ghosts washed away,
washed-up, overseas, submerged.

I can't help but feel connected
to this stranger, this Terry. At first
I was very hesitant about taking his shirts,
being conscious of his son's refusal first.

Yet they fitted me perfectly,
and now they connect me to her too.
Engulfing my torso in the way
I crave to wrap around her.

Was this the shirt he wore
when his heart failed him
in the Caribbean, under a beating sun
in Hell or Barbados?

Did he dance with Wendy his wife in this shirt
holding her close, head pressed on chest,
where her eardrum would beat
to the God-given rhythm pulsing in him

before it stopped? Like I wish her head
was pressed on my chest now. Listening
to my valves opening, forcing this blood,
this oxygen, this breath around me, as once in Terry.

Where did he go? What did he do in it?
Watch *Eastenders*, fish, play cards,
have a shit, eat soup, shave and so forth …
there's so much I don't know and probably never will

now. So I wear this shirt to keep him alive in me,
somehow. Seemingly stitching together some meaning.

BUTCHERY
*for Tim*

'the real Other for the white man is and will continue to be
the black man'
– Frantz Fanon, *Black Skin, White Masks*


I was prepared to kill. I am prepared to kill.
The newly-whetted blade was handed to me
and I made the first incision, only a graze.
Me, the Mzungu under their othering gaze
drew first blood. The sounds made will stay
with me for all my living days.

Only being an apprentice at killing, I expected
the keen edge to glide through the goat's throat.
Instead the raw hide supplied all the resistance of life.
No time for my attempts at a delicate, dignified death,
this only prolonged the pain, the sinew-shudder.
The *coup de grâce* was taken from me graciously, to our relief.

'Charlie', a Maasai warrior wearing a Valencia jersey
became a self-made *conquistador*, executed the deed
with haste. The decapitation complete, I braced myself
for the next step of surgical slaughter. The point of the knife
made its mark down the belly to the anus where shit
like caviar was expelled to the air.

The gases and heat were released from the bowels
as the unfolding of proceedings and skin took place.
Bucking ceased as the plastic tang held
with a new affection now navigated
its way through the cadaver,
with edge dissecting the artery and aorta.
Lungs now breathless are removed, liver and kidneys
are tossed on the heat alongside the heart of Tyrian purple.

The bloodied colours of butchery are scorched to charcoal,
the offal is handed around Oompa Loompa-like. I bite hard,
tearing savagely, forgetting to taste, nothing to savour.
No more grazing, the horizontal pupils have seen
their last of Arusha's grass.
As the carcass is manoeuvred over the flame,
the flies gather
offending my First World sensibilities. Knowing
I still will gorge.

## Teanga/Tongue

'where there's ambiguity, they'll be anglicized'
– Brian Friel

Brian is six years old and from Listowel.
Brian is loved by his parents
Mary and Billy, and his sister Ava.

Brian is into Angry Birds and Star Wars.
Brian is wearing his Kerry GAA PJs,
as proud of his county as his family are of him.

Brian has to go to a special school in Tralee
Mary told me.
Brian has a speech impediment.

Brian has trouble saying 'sweets'.
The 's' and 'w' haven't found his tongue yet,
unlike sugar.

Brian uses the word *milseán*
instead of sweets,
to get what he wants.

Brian has reminded me
of another Brian,
and his *Translations*.

Brian can be provided with all the words.
But he chooses to say what he wants.
How he wants.

Brian's *teanga*
is not tongue-tied.
Brian is 6 years old and from Listowel.

the elderly woman scans the items
as the conveyor belt
relentlessly pushes the pace
she rings the bell
there's some confusion over a reward card
with the woman in front
or something to that effect
the computer says no
all too often
a supervisor comes over
eyes rolling keys rattling
inputs the codes
all resolved for now
nobody means any harm
moments later the bell is rung again
it's just the ...
pace is relentlessly pushed
her name badge displays
the name Jacki
she has a wedding band and simple jewellery
she is more than a scanner of items
but she has checked out
literally and metaphorically
ages ago
who could blame her
her arthritic hands send the items my way
I pack them into my recycled bag
I used to never go to her queue
the slowness frustrating me
not fitting for these modern times
now I ask
what's the rush?
I ask how she is
willing her to look up

connect
take your time
ring that bell if you need to
never mind those
rolling their eyes and rattling keys
Jacki is here
she has made it this far
what have you done?
I am reminded of my Granny James
who once packed bags when she was in her eighties
but before all that she was a seamstress on Harcourt Street
she had four beautiful children
and many grandchildren.
If I deserved it
she would give me Mars bars as a treat.
She deserved the time of day
before she was found at the bottom of the stairs
in her home alone.

'Now did you get all you were looking for?' Jacki asks.
*I did thanks*
and more.
I had to slow things down for a moment
as the pushed pace is relentless.
'Now, anything else?' she says ...

## TICKING CLOCK
*after* Jimmy X *by Mannix Flynn*

Tick ... tick ... ticking clock.
You can't stop the rush to the head
and you can't stop to push instead.

We come through things,
we go through things
which allow us to evolve.

So push through the hymen,
eat the apple,
turn to the preacher and say 'amen'.

Learn to see, to be,
to talk, to walk.
I think, therefore I am another consumer.

Clock's ticking.
Time to comprehend life
and understand the incomprehensible.

Clock's ticking.
Time to communicate
and grow.

What's that?
Cry then to laugh,
cry just for your attention.

I've lost the understanding.
It's all incomprehensible.
Clock's ticking.

Time to find things, to lose things.

Learn life's little rules
or something.

Be good, be bad,
get a kick up the ass,
a slap on the wrist,

a mouth full of soap
and a key to leave home.
But not yet!

Riding around free.
Your own man until
bedtime, dinnertime, anytime.

Get a face full of infection,
an early morning erection,
and a part-time life.

A part-time job.
A part-time man.
Clock's ticking.

Time to be a man, not a boy.
Grow up. Contribute.
Consume.

Plan for the future.
Plan for protection.
Bollocks.

It's only 99% effective.
100% sperm directive.

Clock's ticking.

Time to teach,
to preach
and see me.

I've not even matured,
I'm too young to be a philistine
and too old to last a lifetime.

Join the gym,
a decision
on a whim.

Where's
my protection, my foundation,
my parents?

They're gone.
They're in me.
Well, that's just fucking great!

So settle.
Down. Down.
Now. Now.

Skip some time.
I'm only 69.
So let's get some.

Air Miles,
ceramic tiles,
stocks and shares.

Soil my pants,
grovel for a young romance.
Settle down and recollect.

Down.
Six feet
Down.

Clocks,
tick, tick,
ticking.

I'm sitting in Slattery's Bar, and there's an old man across from me with half a pint in front of him. He has cataracts in his eyes, he checks his watch by ear to hear the passing of time, zips his coat, sinks some pint, sizes me up, I think, senses me somehow, sits straight up, hands with strength search softly for a blind man's cane.

Barman says,
Daniel you ok? Do you need a hand home?

Daniel replies with an inaudible whisper and barman says, sure you're right, you've half a pint in front of you. Despite no sight the weight of the jar is still measured perfectly by his hand. I've an urge to talk to him, yet I want to leave him to his own devices. Daniel coughs a little. I order a pint and think about ordering one for him, but instead I leave him be, and we sit opposite each other for a while, and all in the world is fine for a moment.

Daniel ups and leaves after draining the remains of the pint; the person who offered to get the door got put in their place, as well they might. Daniel walked his way to that door more times than they've darkened it. Barman goes out after him with good intentions. I'm alone now surrounded by strangers, yet knowing I'll be sitting where Daniel was in another forty years and I'm just fine with that.

Barman tells me Daniel is 89 and was born in Mayo. He now lives up the road, cooks all his own meals and is totally blind after being kicked by a horse at the age of 23! I'm only sorry I found out this information second-hand and not from the horse's mouth, as it were; apparently he loves a chat. I should have bought him that pint.

It was upstairs in this very bar going back about eleven years that I recited my first poem in public. Where has the time gone? The journey poetry has taken me on has been epic, and tonight while having a jar by myself the poems are all over the place, they're hanging from the ceiling, dripping from the taps, but mostly living in the eyes and swilling in the mouths of all the souls here, no doubt many a muse still haunts this space. I may as well be at the foot of Parnassus. I should frequent this place more often, it's good to come back to what you know.

So I came back the following Friday seeking pints, poems, but mostly Daniel and he did not disappoint. Never letting on that it was me sitting across from him the previous week, when he appeared we chatted casually, shook hands, exchanged names. I helped him get a stool and he sat in 'his' spot. Mostly though it was about letting him talk, and he did. So I listened.

He was totally blind, so he went to learn braille off a young girl working out in Bray and she asked, 'Daniel, have you worked with cement?' He had as a young man, and the touch of the lime, the calcium carbonate, had scorched him of any sensitivity, the feeling of sight was lost to his fingers from the stacking of brick. So on occasion someone reads the paper to him, or the wireless connects him to other worlds, while other worlds all around me flow in conversation. The fullness of his life, his resilience, even the twinkle still left in his opaque crystalline lens captivates me. Cancer took his wife, his children joined the diaspora, the stories and wisdom of this bar-bound Buddha casts Zen out to all who'll listen. So I listen and look at his hands, at his majestic hands burned to the touch.

*(ditty)*
Daniel has strength in his hands,
Daniel says it'll all be grand,
come now hold our hands,
we understand,
we'll all be grand,
we'll all be grand.

HER HEART OPENED
*commissioned by Concern*
*for Open Heart House*

Her heart opened, singing
with the purity of birdsong
in a room where
too many truths have been spilt.

A small room off Dorset Street,
lit by a skylight,
almost the only escape
for prayers rising,

flying with
many melodies.
The colour of the room
escapes me.

It doesn't matter,
but I am thinking blue
or some other hue
of forgetfulness.

She sits there picking
at an unhealed wound
covered with tattoos
and too many taboos.

She sings again.
I shake, I want to hug
but sometimes distance
is the kindest thing.

Despite the questioning,
despite the un-answers,

despite the betrayal,
despite me not knowing,

never knowing,
pretending to understand,
applying empathy,
nodding my head,

'Sure, yeah, go on'.
'What's your favourite colour?'
I ask. Something
more or less personal,

something real to me,
something I can understand,
fleshing her out.
I don't know her and yet I ask …

'How did it happen?'

She knows we are here for this.
We're prepared for the violence
as much as you can be.
She says as much as she can. She says ...

I'm thinking what is courage?
I'm thinking now I know she is my hero.
She speaks of the birds and the bees,
the hawk and the honey.

That time, aged fourteen,
wanting to impress,
wanting to please
all too much, too much

violence,
violation,
when love
is dangerous.

Some take,
some give,
some got
what they ought not.

Her first child taught her
she had HIV.
Her first moment of joy,
another decoy.

Now when going for testing
at St James's Hospital, no surprise
she seeks disguise,
only going the same day

as the addicted and the convicted.
A place not for her,
but a place of camouflage.
A hidden face.

The melody changes. The tone
of being alone reverberates.
Unable to use the medicine
because of the perceived sin,

the thoughts of letting
him win
makes the room spin.
The skylight shatters

all those things
that are meant to matter.
Go blue and I sink
into the depths of her.

A fear of drowning,
yet we go deeper, refusing
the oxygen we need
and our held breath

won't sustain us
for long and this song
says something
is wrong.

What is brave?
Brave for me
is waking up every morning
and looking prejudice in the eye.

Being warm
in a cold system
and giving the kiss of life
to others

when you have already exhaled.

## NIGHTSKY AND BUTTERFLY

I've done more sleeping here than I'd intended to ...
The other morning when I went to make coffee,
there was a butterfly
that had somehow found its way into the cottage.
I couldn't reach to free it.
So, it stayed there fluttering away,
pressed against the glass.

I sat alone all the day
burning turf, turning pages
and playing with the pine cone
I found on the path.

I looked up at the darkness of the sky,
they say this area is a Dark Sky Reserve,
people come here to gaze.
In-between my navel gazing I saw Orion
hunting in *Star Wars* above the Skellig Islands.
I wonder, during a clear moonless night
would the gables take the weight?

This here is the 'core zone'
of the Dark Sky Reserve.
There is no 'critical light'.
A buffer zone protects this 'core zone'.
This isthmus is reaching beyond
and in the distance
a lighthouse flashing, calling us in.

We love only until we don't.

The next morning the butterfly
landed on me.
I took it in my hand
and led it to the door.

Only in going away
can we realise
where home is ...

## CANAL SWANS

So much intertwined, tangled
and the length of this skein
can only be revealed in the
spanning of a canal swan's wing.

ENCHANTED

The half-light conjures shadows.
A kernel, curving. I wish to caress,
trace-touch, then on towards a tickle,
till all shapes are charmed, a mess
of you and me and light-spell riddle.

## Liminal Space

I'm always:
impure, unclear, esoteric.

You're always:
royally-blessed, Hellenic.

We're not ones to obey.
It's attraction, magnetic.

## METAPHLOWER

The flower
that bloomed
in my hand
was taken by the wind.

The scent may fade. Yet
the memories remain
of fallen pollen
petals.

## WHERE MY SEROTONIN?

Sure it's all
in your head.
Isn't it?

## I HAVE SEEN BEAUTY

But I have also
seen beauty
that wanted to die.

## HUNTER

You have caught
real beauty
like a hunter.
It didn't notice
you coming.

I didn't notice you coming,
but you lured me in, in a trance.
So feminine with your grace
and so feline with pace
in catching your prey.

Helpless, at your mercy.
Nothing left to do but pray
being caught is just
the beginning of the chase,
and not the end of your life.

## Anto for Taoiseach
*for Pat Kinevane*

I'm up too bleeding
early. But I shrugged off
my daily itch, only to be hindered
by my own domestic bitch.
So to re-engineer my
acoustic life only to
still eat porridge. And live
on an antioxidant.
Stress-supplied.
Multi-supplemented
life. So get nude, blend
some chamomile tea.
I'd say that John's only a
dreamer with no religion
and crazy philosophy.
Attract women and talk,
it's easier than it seems.
Grafton Street was walked
on, and I saw Jimmy singing
Hare Krishna at the most expensive
free open air concert
a free man's experienced.
Doorways were pissed
on. Ha'penny was pissed
and gone in the head.
But he contributed,
he fucking contributed,
with the generosity
of a widow's mite!
That man's a legend
in Dublin in my eyes.
To sleep in those doorways
and cast back all the living

that he had to the treasury of life.
It makes me sad, and glad
to see life living in the spirit
of a poor man giving
'cause when I look at him I see just
how futile that life can be,
and how he's richer than D4,
as he puts his fingers up
and lets out a roar
and takes out a smoke
and inhales to choke
in his last days. But he lived
his life like a ciggie
in the rain never fading when
the pain washed in.

*IOMRAMH*
*written at Cill Rialaig, Co. Kerry, thanks to Listowel Writers' Week.*
*In memory of Danny Sheehy (Domhnall Mac Síthigh)*

A man goes to the coast of an island to be alone.
He has gone as far as he can
for now.
It's called retreat.
A great distance is not always far enough
when the mind is as restless as the ocean
you're sleeping beside.

This man is seeking solitude
and in doing so has brought the loneliness
into his own heart.
Sure he knew this would be the way of it,
but he still put one foot in front of the other.
You've to face it,
sometimes learn.

The barren landscape has seen worse.
He reminds himself
of the continued struggle and erosion
that is life.
He thinks that's a cliched metaphor,
a famine village is deserving of more.

He looks out at the ocean all too often,
the primal part of him wanting to rage in the deep blue.
Yesterday was Valentine's Day
and around the table he was told a tragic love story
of a man who, after he buried his love,
climbed to the top of Bolus Head
and threw himself to the depths.

After this story the man made the same trek.
It would be so easy to climb the rock walls,

pass by the sheep in the fields and dive,
never submitting but knowing it's a fight
never to be won
once submerged.
There's something honest in that though
he thinks,
is there?
Never submitting.

Those rocks are patient hunters,
how much violence have they caused by simple stillness?
Then birdsong called through the air,
like so many times it has called him away from a dark edge,
like so many times it is the simple things in his life
that save him, fond memories, curiosity.
He could have sworn
he saw the Fibonacci sequence in a spider web earlier,
this reminded him.
Those rocks can wait for now.
Instead he'll walk into the wind
which numbed his face yesterday
while a warm heart pounds on beneath all the layers.

You can go so far and it's never enough.
You can learn to be still and it'll come to you.

You can think of moving rocks,
battling nature,
or arranging words in some fashion aiming for legacy.
This is redundant.
You fucking know this.
Leave your ego at this pagan peninsula,
echoes of trauma are just that,
time for silence.

You are here.
It's sunny outside.
The man notices the bruise on his knee is fading,
the salted air is already healing.

Later he'll eat eggs and light a fire.
Later good things will come to pass.

He remembers this right now
as he sits still warming his feet
ready to wander …

### DANNY'S TRANSLATION

Téann fear go cósta oileáin chun a bheith ina aonar
tá sé imithe chomh fada agus is féidir leis
fén dtráth seo.
Cúlú a thugtar air!
Is minic ná fuil dóthain i dturas fada
agus an aigne chomh corrathónach leis an bhfharraige go
gcodlaítear taobh léithi.

Tá an fear seo ar thóir aonaránachais
agus is tríd seo a phréamhann uaigneas ina chroí
ach ná raibh a fhios aige go maith gur mar seo a bheadh
ach fós shiúil sé roimis
caitheann tú tabhairt fé uaireanta
foghlaim …

tá i bhfad níos measa feicithe ag an dtírdhreach
neamhthorthúil
meabhraíonn sé dó féin
fén síorstracadh agus creimniú

sin é an saol
ceapann sé go meafar seanachaite é seo
tá níos mó feicithe ag baile gorta

féachann sé ar an aigéan rómhinic
a mhianta bunúsacha á réabadh sa doimhneas gorm
b'é inné Lá Fhéile Bhailintín
agus ag an mbord innsíodh truascéal grá dhó
fén bhfear a dhreap go barra Cheann Bhóluis
agus a rop é féin sa duibheagán
tar éis do a ghrágeal a adhlacadh

thug an fear fén gcosán céanna i ndiaidh an scéil seo
bheadh sé furasta na faillteacha a dhreapadh
thairis na caoire sna goirt agus léimt as do chraiceann
gan géilleadh choíche ach ag tuiscint
gur cath é nach féidir a bhuachtaint
nuair atá sé tumtha
ceapann sé gur rud éigin ionraic é sin áfach
nó an mar sin é?
gan géilleadh choíche

is fiagaithe foighneacha na carraigeacha seo
cé méid foréigin a tháinig as a gciúnas simplí
ansan tháinig cantain éin tríd an aer
fé mar a ghlaoigh siad air go minic ó fhaobhar an bháis
amhail go minic gurbh iad na nithe simplí ina shaol a
shaorann é
cuimhní geanúla, fiosracht,
d'fhéadfadh sé a dhearbhú
go bhfeaca sé Sequence Fibonacci i líontán an damháin alla
níos luaithe
mheabhraigh sé seo dhó
gur féidir leis na carraigeacha seo fanacht mar atáid
siúlóidh sé in ionad san tríd an ngaoith

a d'fhág a aghaidh sioctha inné
faid phreabann croí teolaí féna ghainní

is féidir leat dul méid áirithe ach ní bhíonn dóthain go deo ann
is féidir leat socracht a fhoghluim agus sroisfidh sé tú

is féidir leat cuimhneamh ar charraigeacha soghluaiste
an nádúir ag troid
nó ag eagrú focal i bhfoirmle ag shlánóidh iad
tá sé seo iomarcach
is maith atá fhios agat é
fág do mhóraíocht sa leithinis Cheilteach seo
níl ansan ach macallaí coscracha
am chun ciúnais
anseo atánn tú
tá sé grianmhar amuigh
cíonn an fear go bhfuil an t-at ar a ghlúin ag trá
tá aer na sáile cheana féin á chneasú

íosfaidh sé uibhe níos déanaí agus lasfaidh sé tine
tiocfaidh nithe maithe chun cinn amach anseo

cuimhníonn sé ar sin anois díreach
le linn dó a bheith suite go socair ag téamh a chos
réidh chun dul ar seachrán ...

## PROZAC POSITIVITY
*for all in St Patrick's Hospital*

My six days of Prozac positivity,
well it started with an empty me.
Numbing our problems
and surroundings, we can only try
and cut through our pain,
for hurt, for reality, for
a fresh perspective in
detecting a sombre mentality,
to bi-polar neutrality.
In contrast to a well-oiled machine,
functioning with efficient spark plug electricity.
So I'll arise and go now, and go
to Laracor, where a secret garden will
suck our souls dry some more.
Nourished by living corpses, beautifully
rotting, blossoming and flourishing, in
a world gone mad addicted to weedkiller,
where a neural uptake has resulted in suicide.
So have you set a date to collide with your maker?
Or some demon heartbreaker? If
I flew over the cuckoo's nest would
you shoot me down or set me free?
Well I'm not here to judge, what's right
for you may not be right for me. But
I know now the *Importance of Being Earnest*. It's
taken me twenty-four years to have learnt this.
It's a lesson, a fable, a parable for happiness.
But it's only when you hit your lowest low, that
you can set your sights high on a new goal. So
please follow your intuition, listen to those
voices from within. Follow feelings to freedom.
I understand. I know it's hard.
I know you hurt yourself.

I know the demons by name. So
say hello to them from me. But
please don't fear them 'cause
I know that we can clear them from
your nightmares. I'm here. I'm near,
and you, you make me real. A real
reality is better than a medicated
mentality, moving to mediocrity,
meditating to purity. Prescribe yourself
some happiness! Prescribe joy!
There ain't no good thing ever dies. So
where are you going? Do
you know where you've been? Do
you know you have beautiful eyes?
Look in the mirror.
Look at yourself.
I can tell you're beautiful.
Can you?

## HOW IS SHE?
*for Trudy*

So how is she? Well
it's probably my
most repeated question,
my biggest frustration,
coming from pure intention.

The truth is
I don't know ... or do I?
Well I can't tell. You'll
have to ask her yourself.

Not even the doctor can
actually see the mending,
it all just defies comprehending,
but thanks for the good messages

you intend, you all intend
on sending. Dare I say a tumour
is easier grasped. Furthermore
misunderstood pain is not easily surpassed,

'cause like a broken bone
you can heal the cracks,
but this goes deeper
to the bone ...

The marrow is mourning
the death of a heart,
the vision of an angel,
the intentions of grace,

the prescriptions of a psychiatrist,
the voltage of feeling,

feeling real, is
there anything else?

So thanks, but
I don't think you get it,
well you can't
actually get it.

This experience isn't
for sale, unless your
chemical imbalance
is romancing with the dark side

of being stale,
to the freshness
of normality.
There I said it.

That's what you're meant
to be, normality is the only
comfortable, acceptable
reality for most of thee.

Just because talking
about feelings and
confronting your demons
is too hard. When

the price of freedom
is in the next addiction,
the next purchase of desire,
wanting to feel higher, but

not needing to accept
yourself. I ask you not
how is she, but
how are you?

Now here I am
transcribing my
eternal conflict,
of ignoring a life

of truth, joy and love
to consume some
ideal that society has
bought into. So

let's show gratitude,
a positive attitude and
release your demons
to heal yourself.

So you're hearing
me preach to communicate
and converse, but
the only experience worth

taking from this is,
how does it
make you feel?
So how is she?

Does her heart pulse?
Can her eyes see?
Can she hear your words?
Does she feel emotions? Yes. And

is she getting better?
Well I feel it was
her experiences that
made her sick, per se.

So can we heal her?
Yes, but only
with love. She will
always remember, but

these moments forever
more are what count.
So is she alive?
I fucking know so.

She lives in a world where
the colours have a taste,
and sometimes there
is so much beauty

it's just hard to
let it all in.
So these are
just my words,

I'm trying to express my feelings,
I'm confronting my
demons and emotions.
You should try it.

You should love
yourself too!
So how is she?
No forget about that …
How are you?

X MARKS
*for Dr Jones*

X marks the spot
and this Mark
has what it's got
to be my brother
from another mother.

The story starts in Montessori school days, between
building blocks, acrylic paints and other childish plays. A
friendship was forged as we gorged on pizzas, racing as
we forced slices of margaritas into juvenile mouths, crust
and all, over Italian dough and football, trust was rising
and a team formed.

Same school, but you were a year ahead, which led me to
learning beyond my years. I was all ears as you'd pass
down nuggets of knowledge so I'd a leg up in school, only
later realized you weren't all that cool, a 'Pool fan through
and through. So LFC became the team for me.

You were always good at the ball though left back was
your role, back to the goal always looking forward,
defensively minded, nullifying attacks and protecting me
off the pitch too.

Got into a hitch,
well a few,

out in Bray one day. Drinking not thinking, flagons, cans,
skipping the last day of summer school promenading on
the seafront promenade, until a bunch of bigger boys,
harder, madder, split my lip in a tussle. You jumped in a
fusilier fusing our bond deeper. And that was the year of
'96, summer time was NHL and 'Mortal Kombat' on Sega
Mega Drive bashing buttons to stay alive. Scorpion was

my character of choice with a 'Get Over Here' and 'Finish Him' we executed all our cares away.

As our teens moved on ... so our keenness in girls grew strong. Apprehensive at best in teenage discos where almost anything goes. How many you'd get? 8 ... I kissed 14! I'd be seen as the shy one, but on the dance floor all my cares would go, me in my Joe Bloggs top and Eclipse jeans ripped at the seams as my growing pains altered my aims. Carpooling home, picked up by parents, roaming through the happenstances but never happening to tell the whole truth to them ...

when we just
want to tell them
all now.

So where one day you got a porno, God knows? I was left shocked with an inflated cock, not so long ago Cheetara of the Thunder Thunder ThunderCats was the only pussy I'd known. However this was just another cartoon, a caricature, and due to the visuals depicted on this screen. We'd so aptly titled these 'absence' interactions *The Simpsons* in permanent black marker on VHS tape, so to escape any parental detection of our bounty of booty!

The best summer I ever had was in Trabolgan, County Cork when it took my mother five hours to drive us down. She'd a nervous breakdown due to a broken-down car and no matter how far that could have pushed you, you knew I needed that holiday. As we played Thin Lizzy on the jukebox with *The Boys Are Back in Town* blaring while shooting pool,

I'd knock
down
another
game ball.

Once,
you were
a bit too game and all,
a blacker side came out and I could have sunk you. I'd
cued up a few thoughts after you swerved your way in to
kiss Annie C, a French girl fond of me. The night previous
I made a bollix of myself, drank too much, drowned in self
doubt. Needing the Dutch courage to clutch at any hope of
getting a French kiss from the Gallic girl. Instead *sacré bleu*!
Excuse my tongue … I was too young to consume such
quantities and ended on my knees vomiting across your
abode; such quantities flowed that you'd to clean up. I
guess I owed you one but to swoop on my *papillon* was in
my eyes wrong and I'm still a little sore about it
but
we'll
move on …

You always had your head between pages, your
household bound up in stacks of hardbacks. Mother and
sister attacking the political talk of the day. I'd sit back,
take it all in, learning to debate and on occasions lobbing
in a curveball to gain reaction, my deliberate jibes always
gaining traction, I'd be rolling on the floor, trolling,
laughing.

Until
your reading

got you
to booking
paths anew
and wherever it took you
I'd a new floor for me to meet, be it Tübingen, Florence or
Rome you had a new beginning, moving forward, looking
at the past, a historian, recording your thought to teach
others, an educator you always were as I found myself
who
knows
where,
living in the past,
scared of the future.
So I found myself into poetry,
my release, and in you I could share a word or two. No
mocking, just ears listening, I'm forever grateful, your
giving of time,
listening to my hammed rhyme
as it helped me to find my own journey
into
others' books,
into
others' ears ...

Now,
we're smashing glass ceilings
again together
striving in our own fields,
if not the best, to be just better.

Do you remember I smashed the garage window? And
Stuart, your auld man, a reserved person, a son of a
preacher from whom I've learned some, kindly forgave me
with a 'we've all done it, it's part of growing up, son', and

with that act my respect he'd won, and, as we bared the
weight of your mum's coffin pressing down on us, life's
circle rotated once again.
That day
we embraced
outside St Anne's
together
we were
at the mercy
of God's plans.

And I've
no idea
how
you, Heather, Stuart and clan held strong, a happy sad that
I got to say my goodbye. Lo and behold she remembered
me, Little Stevie Wonder Boy. It struck me what it might
have been like for the family to home care, witnessing
firsthand how the government doesn't do enough became
clear to answer the needs of those suffering from cancer.
It's important you know, I'm always here,
I'm
here
always.

So now every time I hear *The Boys are Back in Town*, I'm
reminded of that summer holiday
and how
all of us
are just
searching in some way.

So if X marks the spot
the thing I've got
is a friendship treasured.

## No Other Words
*for all in Cheeverstown House*

Darren
says 'car'. He has
no other words, no
words like 'love'.

Darren
likes ice-cream
on Bray seafront
on a windy day.

Darren
will break
your heart.
He never meant to,

he never
knew he
did or could
again.

Darren
says car.
It is not all he means.
It is not all he needs.

Darren
is 13. He will
never be older,
despite appearances.

For him
loved ones don't
reside, so the
givers give love.

One day he let
me touch his face.
He never let anyone.
He rested his head

on my chest, I dared
not to move. I froze,
I broke, I could
not take his kindness!

Darren
looks out from
behind the veil
of his window

as I
drive off
into
my world.

Darren
says
car.

He
   has
      no
         other
            words …

## To Paint this Picture
*Commissioned for RTÉ's* Reality Bites

To paint this picture
I'm going back sure,
ten years to twenty-one.
Young man, inexperienced,
just having fun. A fumble,
previously just a friendly touching of bum.

She, she was otherworldly, blonde, Ukrainian, no head
wreath worn, warm though she was my sunflower. Anya
her name. Yeah we tarried for about six weeks. May as
well have been Áine, the Celtic goddess of love.

On this precipice, no peer pressure for me. I was ready to
bid *adieu* to hesitation, tired of being my own master of
bation. The fear of blindness gone, it was time for me to
open my eyes to see ... hands and parts enfolding, us
tasting sex, mist lifting, vapours entwining, no need for
cupid, cauldrons, cherry blossom puns, pheromones, gods
of love, my devilish angel sent from above had clouded
my mind where I mistook sheer lust as love.

Her, my pillion passenger on back of moped as I sped
from Crumlin to Tallaght, blessed by the gods, hallelujah
at our arrival. My home empty as others holidayed. We
relaxed, swayed to the music, breathing in the air, album
*Moon Safari* playing in background. Track 2: 'Sexy Boy'.
Track 3: 'All I Need' ... Remember, *You Make it Easy*, lucky
lyrically it was all coming together ...

Then, scenario! A hitch, no protection a barrier. So on toe,
to the local, the jacks, the johnny machine and bingo. Just a
foreplay stumble rectified by some uttering,
a mumble. And it became time ...

We weren't spooning, we fit like Lego building,
where between her legs I go, enveloped,
just as much as entering the forbidden flesh. Touching
with eyes closed, letting go of childish ways.

An offering in parts. My heart,
not knowing anything like this before. It was all-good,
sure, time goes backwards on these waters, and crash
and waves on seas. 'Le Voyage de Pénélope', I'd hoped
I'd be her Ulysses yet I was still blind to eventual
probabilities … Until, *ne me quitte pas, ne me quitte pas* …

You left, me heartbroken. We'd planned to do so many
things together my sunflower. You told me your favourite
painting was Pablo Picasso's 'Still Life with a Mandolin'.

It's said to be a night scene in which a fruit dish, bottle and
mandolin are displayed on a table covered
by a white-striped red cloth. All the objects are painted
in a rhythmic and balanced order with lush plain colours
and different pattern motifs.

For a few years after our night scene, I'd go
to the Gallery, thinking of our exhibition,
I'd sit there for up to an hour
staring at this image.
There is
a copy of it
on the wall
of my childhood
bedroom
now
hanging, since.

While we
may not have been
picture perfect,
that moment
I was captured.

I came back home to open dusty shoeboxes and unveil
dusty memories for this poem. And, as time has passed,
the thing that stands out most in my mind is the letter you
left behind the following morn. The one in which you
simply said I 'looked so beautiful while sleeping' and if
that is the memory you too have from the fruits of our
labour,

I've no regrets,
no
regrets
at all.

## Andrew after School

Shortcutting St Joseph's
tonight, a schoolyard where
I often stop to admire
the children's artwork
in windows.

Next to the graffiti
attempts by teens
I also admire,
creating as they kiss,
piss and spit on grounds.

I'm transported
back to twenty years
ago, sitting in a car
waiting for Andrew
after school.

He was soft, mild,
olive-skinned,
often smiled,
wiped-off by me
as a child.

Tonight in Joe's
where I admire
childish ways,
I am sorry Andrew
for my foolish days.

Patron of the dying,
patron of the just,
let my hubris be deflating,
and Andrew again
in me trust.

## HIS SHIELD HIS CRUTCH
*for the Smyths*

He keeps a poem
in his pocket
to echo back
to withstand the storm
to chant the great unspoken

to reach out and shatter
that. That which is most Irish.
He keeps a poem
in his pocket
to harbour love.

Why this poem?
This poem is for him.
This poem was delivered
unexpectedly. It cast aside
all the times when

a pint would suffice,
a public declaration,
an ode thought over,
brewed for years,
compressed and suppressed,

hidden, then
revealed among
folded pages
bringing you back
to 1986,

to grassy fields.
When showing,
not telling
is all that mattered.

NO REASON
*for Anya*

Я счастлив
(I am happy)
when you are.
Я счастлив
when you are.

There, there's
no reason for you to feel this way,
but yet you feel it
for no reason.

What do you feel?
I wish I could touch it,
pour my heart onto a sleeve
and put a needle through it.

It's a creeping angel,
blowing in
and out.
That's the truth of it.

So how does the ironic graph go?
Hurt versus pleasure, sadomasochistic flow,
please sir, can I have
some more?

The Liffey it completely disappeared
under floating buildings.
I'm here. It's happening.
Sorry Thom.

And a near full moon
cascaded over SIPTU

where I'll ask the trade unions,
what on earth to do?

And give something more.
Just to have it sucked dry
by a smile. And accept
that you hope, that my hope,

will self-destruct.
Ah, well you know
we're all fucked
if you don't love forever!

VISITING OR STAYING IN THAT PLACE
after *Krapp's Last Tape*

Remembering too much of the forgotten.
Selected memories.

Remembering daisy chains, smuggling champagne
on New Year's Eve, cubical sex, cut wrists.

So much laughter disguising,
empathising cuts deeply, then, now.

Baggage compartmentalised, all being finalised,
her eyes rolling, blinding.

Now remembering you not remembering. A name.
After your shock, our electrocution.

'How is she?' asked everyone.
Remained unanswered.

Dumb.
Numb.

## LITTLE MITE
*for Cormac in Paris*

Cormac came over
to me,
treading tenderly,
trembling slightly.

Had something to say,
to me,
that he's been carrying,
bursting from within him,

too long, all too short.
No small talk here,
paternal fears spoken
as we opened up to each other.

This is not what we
were expecting,
after a performance.
this is where

pleasantries exchange.
Instead, he said his truth,
as I'd said mine on stage.
No theatrics here.

No applause sought.
Just two men talking,
after three men talking.
And some terrible beauty is born.

'Stephen,
after 39 days

we lost our child.
Miscarried'.

What a word.

All the embers of your love
cannot be carried incorrectly.
They can only burn too quickly
in unimaginable love.

Your love Cormac
is inextinguishable.
Your little mite Cormac
is always in you.

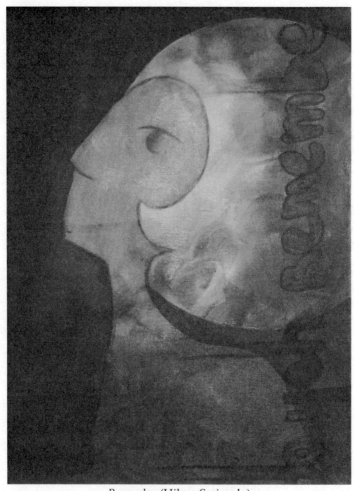

*Remember* (Hilary Seriously)

## I'VE HAD LOVERS

I've had lovers
and I've had loves ...

but when I love again,
I will love like Michael Furey.

Is it unrealistic to love
like a fictional character?

Who's been conjured up
in the mind of Jimmy,

a young Traveller who serenaded
his love in the dead of winter,

his lungs frozen
with a snowy song of ache,

unable to rest with the yearning
to proclaim.

I want to proclaim
all my love with fury.

I'm done with
tepid encounters.

Sparks and dying embers
only warm the souls in passing.

Flames can only extinguish
lost feelings burning me up.

Let's not insult each other
with kind kisses.

Let's tear out our hearts
or nothing at all!

*Galway Seagull* (Tiffany Choong)

BRING IT HOME
*commissioned by AVIVA for the IRFU*

As clubs, counties, provinces unite,
we set forth on our excursion, crossing borders
and class divides ready for the fight!
A brief incursion with Wanderers from
sportsgrounds Thomond, Ravenhill, Donnybrook,
trying to bring it home and evoke Invictus with a bit of luck.

Bringing it home for more than an acronym IRFU,
doing it for the crowd, me and you,
singing voices aloud with 'manic aggression' and control,
we are the Best captains of our unconquerable soul.

With swirl of faces, flags and emerald jerseys,
we remind the mind of 'the fear of God',
the style of Kyle, BOD, Briggs
eccentric scoring Axeled around the
endurance of one-way thinking.

We remember the wooden spoons, Triple Crowns,
knock-ons, knock backs, forward passed,
battle cries of 'I'll play for you all day',
rosary praying, clichéd sayings, dropped chances
and perfect Parisian drop goals, future folklore yet untold.

We take the glory of 1948, 2009, 2013 and
we take Stockdale in the team of 2018
where we can all dream, even Gary Breen,
of a team answering 'Ireland's Call',
to swing low and pluck that Saxon foe, a Rose,
after Azzurri, Dragon, Thistle and Gallic *coq*
bringing it home on Paddy's Day won't be such a shock!
Bring it back home to our Pantheon, our palindrome,
sure we always say we're 'grand'
time to prove it and Slam it home!

## An Ode to Tony McMahon's Den

I was strolling the streets of The Coombe,
Dublin's celestial womb,
I'd the hunger in my belly
and me legs were goin' jelly.
I was in search of a bite,
when by chance on Francis Street
Libby and her little sis Ruth I did meet.
'What brings round you here?' I say.
'Ah did you not hear?' they say.

Come gather round and listen
there's a Rambling House beginning
Kerry's descended upon Dublin
in Tony McMahon's den …

When we open up to chance,
we'll know the way.
When we know the way
we'll dance ...

So I ambled onwards,
towards this Rambling House,
passing markets for horses, hops
and oh there the heroine
auld Anne Devlin,
muralled by Maser,
having strolled these streets herself
in bygone days sure.
I wonder what verse Vincent Caprani
would pen for the oncoming Gaiety
then just off Gray Street.
My comrades I did greet
for this was a party of
pipers, poets, paupers
and Workers Party politicians.

This wasn't Inniskeen Road
but it was a July evening.
This wasn't Billy Brennan's Barn
but the bicycles were aligning,
leaning up against stone walls
where geraniums were hanging
either side of the doorway
where I sat on the wooden floor
a throne for this castaway.

When we open up to chance,
we'll know the way.
When we know the way
we'll dance ...

Steve says 'what'll we start with?'
Not me, another Steve, a myth.
And we're off.
And on!
Jigs, reels, polkas, tunes,
no song.

I open
my eyes and ears wide.
You sense the pride!
There's
gas laughs and by-gollys hysteria,
gas lamps from bygone eras,
cobwebs catching the light,
I spy a spider slowly, silkily, descending into an air
built on its own might.
There's
dusty bookshelves and Parisian paintings taking us away ...
There's
writing desks, step-ladders,

ironing boards and not a word, just the tunes heard.
young and old ears,
tuned to an ancient pitch
4-32 a tone your grandparents and Verdi knew.
Every key further unlocks this open house,
the pendulum on the clocks even stopped
but it's right twice a day.
This is The Pure Drop,
no lips go parched,
and some are even puckering up
for the mistletoe still hanging in the kitchen!
Buddha gazes on, spreading good karma,
bulbs blown don't dim thanks Jah,
I'd a chinwag with Ita from Cabra.
Beside the fireplace there's an aloe vera plant,
and I can't even begin to thank the world for this blessing.
There's a ringing in our ears and bare feet are tapping
while rain lightly taps along in time on the windowpane.
No hurt here for now, no pain for now …
I abstained from
the overwhelming offers of sandwiches
but with a China tea cup
I toast to Tommy Potts a fiddler and fireman,
aptly over the fireplace and I swig a sup,
for those not here for the *blás*.
The fairy music is flowing and I'm all *athas* with living,
we're all alive,
as the spirits arise, to share this space.
The White Lady is in window
and the blue-haired woman is in the corner.
As Gaels speak the *teanga isteach sa teach*
*agus amach, amach*, outside, outside
outside of me
a tear rolls down my face,
as sweat pours down Cormac's concertina.

He plays within himself,
honouring us in this outer realm.
A raven bellowing out beautiful airs of Blasket boatmen.
We are taken there,
we are no longer here
in this room
in Dublin's Liberties.
We are at prayer
in church
just around the corner from Vicar Street
ascending all the concrete,
atune to a new frequency,
and frequently we are
out of our hearts,
of ourselves.
We are liberated
and we vibrated to each other,
for we have to move.
For I have been moved.
Each movement a ripple.
I am in no fixed state,
when I say I,
I mean we.
We can't stop now.
Take it all in,
and let everything out.
Go.
We'll never be able again.
It won't end here,
here now,
without you.
We are on the air.
A spider slowly, silkily, descending into an air,
casting on invisible waves ...

C'mere you were told,
bring a bottle and your ears to the affair,
get there early or you'll be lucky to get a chair!

Come gather round and listen
there's a Rambling House beginning.
Kerry's descended upon Dublin
in Tony McMahon's den …

When we open up to change,
we'll know the way.
When we know the way
we'll not feel strange …

When we open up to chance,
we'll know the way.
When we know the way
we'll dance …

*A Playful City* (Shane Sutton)

*A Playful City* (Shane Sutton)

FROM ... TO ...
*Street art commission for* A Playful City *with Shane Sutton*

From a rite of passage
> to a bowl of porridge.

From Happy Slappings
> to inappropriate Snapchat happenings.

From dead legs
> to six feet under.

From The Circle Game
> to it being your round.

From apple drops
> to double drops.

From Refresher bars
> to refresher courses.

From winner winner chicken dinner
> to gis a go of your fidget spinner.

From kiss-chasing
> to the rat racing.

From mommies and daddies
> to doctors and nurses.

From discotheques twerking
> to ballroom dancing.

From pushing swings
> to swigging flagons.

From Tip the Can
> to *Puff the Magic Dragon.*

From cartoons on TV
> to junk food in grams and keys.

From cops and robbers
> to shooting up.

From Terrible Twos
> to ASBOs.

From Manhunt
> to gunmen.

From 3 and in
> to 3 and 1s.

From it's 1 for all
> to it's all 4 one.

From seesaws
> to suicides.

From Snakes and Ladders
> to stairway to heaven.

From the Children of Lir
> to homeless kids here.

From Dustin the Turkey
> to burnt Christmas dinners.

From jumpers for goalposts
> to frapping Facebook posts.

From St Vincent de Paul
> to *Adam and Paul*.

From British Bulldog
> to IRA.

From hide and seek
> to a constructive critique.

From Wendy House
> to wet houses.

From skateboarding
> to waterboarding.

From pony trekking
> to bareback riding.

From running errands
> to becoming parents.

From first memories
> to Alzheimers.

From playing marbles
> to losing them.

From Humpty Dumpty
> to being called a numpty.

From Truth or Dare
> to dare I tell you?

From starter nappies
                 to starter homes.
From umbilical cords
                 to bungee cord.
From Roger Rabbit
                 to *Playboy* bunnies.
From Hopscotch
                 to scotch-on-the-rocks.
From Lego bricks
                 to selfie-sticks.
From dinosaur toys
                 to App store buys.
From candy apples
                 to Candy Crush.
From sticks and stones
                 to broken bones.
From cyberbullying
                 to accountability.
From astronauts
                 to headspace.
From stargazing
                 to centralizing.
From no stress
                 to mindfulness.
From breastfeeding
                 to recycling.
From prosperity
                 to reality.
From wonder
                 to doubt.
From baby wipes
                 to bottom lines.
From development
                 to growth.

From private

                    to public.

From being named

                    to being anonymous.

From learning to speak

                    to learning to listen.

From the past

                    to the future.

From young

                    to old.

From you

                    to me.

From fearful

                    to playful.

## HAIKU

You never call back.
Are the satellites working?
Our orbits break free ...


I've just landed, and
nobody can tell if I'm
bird, plane, *Superman* ...


Ignition ignites
heart beats, joy rides, some mothers
laying roadside wreaths


There's a mountain Who,
with a mighty view, which is
why we try hike Who!


My X iPhone knows,
MyFaceLocationSecrets!
Techno. Love. Matrix ...


If anyone asks
I was never here ok?
We see what we want

My mum took me here
a lot has happened since then
what will be will be ...


I wish you were here
Moscow is so far away
I feel you so close.


I'd like to kiss her
but then I thought about you
all you mean to me.


I feel so much love
for my students, I want to
protect and let go ...


Ballymun buskin'
Dublin streets echo with pride
committed artist


Boats afloat off coasts
smile for fire-water toasts
Danny drinks oceans

A public promise
sworn to give all forever
you are family


Beautiful newborn
could in time have the power
to rape, love, hurt, heal


I didn't like school
nobody knew who I was
and neither did I


I love these children
I am going to miss them
the future is theirs


Slimy snail suckin'
on a stone, so I see if
it'd like some sea salt ...


Thanks for the invite
to share my understanding
that comes from the heart

We all have a price.
I have just discovered mine.
Do I have a soul?


Flame-grilled summer flesh,
BBQ smell in the air ...
yummy E-Coli!


I like the back row
of the cinema, with you.
Popcorn gobstoppers!


Your criticism
when you don't know the context
means nothing to me.


Dandelion springing
for sunshine, sway yellow heads
looking for the light ...


I toast gone-off bread
two days past the best thing since
it has come to this

Those that can't do teach
I'll try to teach what I do
sharing is the way ...


The apple blossoms
in my garden remind me
of my mother's hands


The degree I got
was not what I expected
I am still learning


Candyfloss for one
the Ferris wheel all alone
spins for me for you

### After John Spillane

Cherry trees blossom,
we have gone around the sun.
Pink petals wind run ...


### On Good Friday 2018

The pubs are open,
go out and have a few pints ...
it's what Jesus wants!

NINE NINE LINES
*inspired by Paula Meehan's 'The Gift'*

*in memory of Paul Curran*

*commissioned by* Poetry Ireland *for #PoetryDayIRL2018*


*I wrote the first faint line emerging,*
within a personal renaissance.
Divined by an owl's hoot, a calling
from Neruda, I formed my response.
Unsure where it would lead me, and still
I'm in awe of the geomantic
marks that unearth some symbolic will.
Oh the mind's magic at times tragic,
please make, *the art that never gets made …*

*My Ireland* (Steve Simpson)

## MY IRELAND
*commissioned by the St Patrick's Day Festival*
*for Sorcha Fox*

My Ireland you are
the river rush
always fluid in flux
in need of a little hush.
My Ireland is talking to itself
but so busy listening to Joe
it's not hearing anything!
My Ireland is saying
*grá go deo agus sláinte Diageo.*
My Ireland is *Reeling in the Years*
and not watching what's happening now
while so many are reining in the tears
and trying to cope somehow.
My Ireland is terrified of leaving the immersion on
and lamenting not having won the Eurovision
in God only knows how long.
My Ireland loves laughing at Ó Briain and Norton.
My Ireland is sending gifs and emojis
while waiting for absolution.
My Ireland needs
a vision, an *aisling*,
to move on from:
bacon and cabbage,
potatoes, leprechauns,
and jaysis *Mrs Brown's Boys*!
My Ireland is checking itself
after a queen's Nobel Call
and in Dublin Castle heard
*a Úachtaráin agus a chairde*
from auld Lizzy.
My Ireland is dizzy from misinformation
and celebrations arising from The Proclamation.

My Ireland wonders if it's a sovereign people
still under the shadow of a steeple?

My Ireland constantly asks:
'was it for this?' and
*an bhfuil cead agam dul go dtí an leithreas?*
My Ireland is Zig and Zag
and top shelf mags,
Pearse lonely as an old woman
defiant in defeat.
My Ireland is a white flag
and Elizabeth O'Farrell's feet.
My Ireland is Savita needing agency,
the Magdalene Laundries.
My Ireland is hysterical
and in denial of being patriarchal.
My Ireland didn't Wake the Feminists,
Queen Maeve was an early riser.
My Ireland you are:
Cumann na mBan
praying to St Brigid,
Ireland playing frigid
Naysayers and Peig Sayers.
My Ireland is still Hailing Mary Mother of Grace,
And here's to you Mrs Robinson thanks for the embrace.
My Ireland wishes Grace O'Malley our Pirate Queen
could've been out at Shell to Sea.
My Ireland is cherishing anything
from an Instagram snap of a
ham and cheese toasty
to finding the right filter
for taking that selfie.
My Ireland is rich land
dressed by Penneys.

My Ireland is *The Quiet Man*
and *Waterford Whispers*,
shouting for us all.
My Ireland isn't sure what to do about
the water charges
and needs someone to take the fall.

My Ireland you are
the river rush of the
Corrib, Nore,
Foyle, Suir, Shannon,
Lagan, Liffey, Lee
and every tributary.
Wash over me,
wash over me,
wash over me ...

My Ireland should learn from its rivers
and burst its banks.
My Ireland needs to go back to the source,
the initial trickle, a spring
and tickle out its flow.
My Ireland needs to let go.
My Ireland saw Sinéad rip up the Pope
and isn't able to cope.
So we've:
Pieta House, Apollo House, Pelican House
for our new age blood sacrifice
and ghost estates.
My Ireland doesn't know what a tracker mortgage is
and is hoping it's not too late.
My Ireland sees goodness,
in the kindness
of its people everyday
which bonds us

just enough to get by.
My Ireland's sense of community
isn't ready to die!
My Ireland celebrates the underdogs
who 'Pull Like a Dog'.
'We're not here to take part, we're here to take over!'
My Ireland you are:
The Guildford Four,
Rossport Five,
Birmingham Six,
Travelling people
and forgotten demographics ...
My Ireland is a terrible beauty,
*agus mol an óige agus tiocfaidh sí.*
My Ireland knows,
'When all the others were away at Mass'
there was *The Meeting on the Turret Stairs*.
My Ireland can let go of all its cares,
it has the arts.
We've The Salmon of Knowledge
and blistered hearts.
My Ireland has warriors like
Damien Dempsey singing 'Colony'
and Katie Taylor knocking out misogyny!
My Ireland doesn't forget to pour a sup for the fairies
and our women's fairy tales sail to Holyhead.

My Ireland you are
the river rush of the
Corrib, Nore,
Foyle, Suir, Shannon,
Lagan, Liffey, Lee
and every tributary.

Wash over me,
wash over me,
wash over me ...

My Ireland can be hard to take,
asks, 'Did St Patrick banish all the snakes?'
My Ireland is the Children of Lir, Tír na nÓg
a herd of deer and a Connacht brogue.
My Ireland is singing,
*Óró sé do bheatha abhaile*, while
the Eastern Europeans are coming,
the Africans are coming,
the Muslims are coming.
Can we all just come together?
My Ireland you are the National Stud.
My Ireland you are:
Four Green Fields
and a clover,
transgender,
other,
Othered,
he,
she,
non-defined,
unexplained,
yet to emerge,
fluid queers.
My Ireland may be drunk on 800 years!
My Ireland is the undocumented
and forty million worldwide.
*Failte* them *abhaile*.
Open your arms.
Do you care about your diaspora?
My Ireland is: West Brits, expats, immigrants,
Shane McGowan, Tipp via London Town.

Ireland you are:
the Kilburn Road, Ellis Island,
Boston, To Hell or Connacht,
Dubai, Oz and Canada.
Skyping to your Da and Ma
My Ireland's calling ...
*Tiocfaidh ár lá!*
My Ireland is pulling the Aran wool over Yankee eyes,
while thanking its bus drivers since 1916.
My Ireland is worried that
Dustin the Turkey and The Rubberbandits
deserve more plaudits for speaking the truth.
My Ireland is fearful of the litigious.
My Ireland is a religious delirious crowd
and Synging playboys,
in a post-truth western world ...
My Ireland is full of notions,
revelations framed in song
and the constellations of a plough
under which we all belong.
My Ireland is Gerard Donnelly resting in the Phoenix Park
as Wellington's obelisk looms in the dark.
My Ireland is Glendalough, Lough Derg,
skirmishes, Skellig Islands and *Star Wars*.

My Ireland you are
the river rush of the
Corrib, Nore,
Foyle, Suir, Shannon,
Lagan, Liffey, Lee
and every tributary.
Wash over me,
wash over me,
wash over me ...

My Ireland, oh my,
you are Omagh!
Danny Boy in Loftus Road,
Good Friday, Bloody Sunday.
An island in Trouble in shock
caught in the crosshairs of a Glock.
My Ireland is
*tír gan teanga*
*tír gan anam,*
and hiding ammunition.
You are white in division,
all sides aiming for some Union ...
My Ireland you are:
a Peace Bridge in Strokestown,
a battle for some,
the Battle of Somme,
a Rising,
a Lily,
a Poppy,
a speech at Woodenbridge,
Others talkin' of leaching on Jobsbridge.
Ireland *is feidir linn!*
Oh yes we can, oh no you can't.
My Ireland's a Gaiety panto.
My Ireland's got the fear
wondering why are we here?
Looking for a pot of gold under
the Cliffs of Moher.
My Ireland's postmodern,
self aware, more than a list poem!
Wandering like Bloom through
the Slieve Bloom and Mourne Mountains.
My Ireland is
Carrickfergus, Carrickmines,

the Ring of Kerry, Boyne Valley,
Bunclody, Enniscorthy.
My Ireland you are:
waterways, wildlife, curlew.
You are:
a *seanchaí* lament,
a Celtic Phoenix,
perpetual hubris.
Ireland you're not one to complain,
*Níl aon tinteán mar do thinteán féin ...*
My Ireland is
taking the soup,
dropping the 'O'
do you feel emancipated?
My Ireland you are:
Bosco knocking on a magic door
Zebo and the Haka in Thomond Park.
You are:
birdsong from a Lark,
Fenians, farmers, freemasons,
executions at Kilmainham Jail,
you are UN peacekeeping
and speak of The Pale after
kissing the Blarney Stone.
My Ireland wherever you roam,
you are always a Paddy, a Biddy, a Mick,
hailing from a Banana Republic.
My Ireland is getting the ride in Copper Face Jacks
and made Big Jack an honorary Irishman.
My Ireland is Anglo Irish
and playing GAA for the parish.
My Ireland is *Glenroe* and Joanne O'Riordan.
My Ireland you are
and aren't the Vitruvian male

and you're up for sale
at the right price.
My Ireland is
the lovely girls at the Rose of Tralee,
Mount Rose and TV3.
My Ireland will gobble you up!
It's obsessed with:
Clonakilty black pudding,
Superquinn sausages,
bottom feeders,
Hunger Strikes,
1798 and pikes,
Black and Tans,
yips and yurts,
scapegoats, drive-bys,
fiscal crisis, Jesus, ISIS,
The Irish Elk, Ireland help!
Ireland, viral, Titanic, epidemic,
from Normans to Neither/Norism.
My Ireland is Archbishop John Charles McQuaid,
enough said!

My Ireland you are
the river rush of the
Corrib, Nore,
Foyle, Suir, Shannon,
Lagan, Liffey, Lee
and every tributary.
Wash over me,
wash over me,
wash over me ...

My Ireland has erased
the Famine, the Great Hunger, the Emergency.
Let's not write our epitaph until we're all free.

My Ireland had a Centenary and got D.P.
My Ireland couldn't look its signatories in the eye.
My Ireland's
ditties and songs,
sure we'll all sing along,
while Louis Walsh looms
and wooden spoons
cause national trauma.
My Ireland is saying RIP Billo,
and knows Dunphy's a spoofer.
My Ireland's trying to survive on the dole
and livin' off of chicken fillet rolls.
Ireland you are:
Happy Pears and Apple accounts.
Ireland you are still living in the past,
how long can this last?
Do you even understand Peadar Kearney's words?
Ireland invented by Declan Kiberd,
revived by Lady Gregory,
wants a portrait from Colin Davidson
but is scared of what it'll see ...
Ireland you are:
Some woman's yellow hair,
Marty Morrissey's hair,
EU fishing quotas,
banker bonuses,
*Paddy Clarke Ha Ha Ha*, Enya,
Eircodes, uilleann pipes,
NAMA and the HSE,
a biscuit and stout industry,
Riverdance, the Walls of Limerick,
private islands, apologies,
Bog Poems, Blackberry-Picking, fermenting,
Wild Geese, Web Summits, Harps,
*Jimmy X, All Kinds of Everything,*

caught in a whirlpool spin.
You are part of the world,
look out
and
look within ...
Mise Éire, Ireland, Hibernia,
you are all this
you are all this
and more!
My Ireland you are
trying to be all encompassing
and it's an impossible task.
So I ask you,
'what's your My Ireland?'
Ireland are you evolving,
arising, an *aisling*,
remembering,
Ireland arise!
Ireland from what I've heard
a great compassion
is calling you.
You have a *teanga*,
so add your voice.
Ireland from what I know
a great courage
is in you.
So stand united rejoice.
Go back to the source, the flow,
forget mainstream.
Let out a roar,
I want to hear you scream:
'This Ireland is my land.

This Ireland is your land.
This island is our land.'

And know I love you.
And know I love you.
I love you.
*Sin é!*

I'm trying to listen,
so what have you to say?

My Ireland you are
the river rush of the
Corrib, Nore,
Foyle, Suir, Shannon,
Lagan, Liffey, Lee
and every tributary.
Wash over me,
wash over me,
wash over you,
wash over us …

## Relit Flame

I've taken myself back to church. Not that
I've faith in Rome or any other destination.
Nor do I seek the spectacle of ceremony.
I come here to be alone in the undergrowth,
to feel small, to pare back with back on
wooden bench. I've come to sacrifice an ego.

Harry Clarke's glass is overhead
glowing with Gabriel's Annunciation.
I'm enriched by the depth of his blue.
Frostlike my divergence came to pass
so long ago, but what road now …
Where am I going to go?

*Flower* (Tiffany Choong)

*The Poet* (Karen Hickey)

Special thanks to my friends and family who have supported me over the years: Aaron Copeland, Ambassador Adrian O'Neill, Aidan Murphy, Aimée van Wylick, Alan Hayes, Alexia Bartlett, Helena Mulkerns, Alison Lyons, Andrea Keogh, Andrej Kapor, Angela Dorgan, Anna Jacob, Andrea Keogh, Aoife Woodlock, Anto Kane, Andy Early, Babs Daly, Barry 'Jazz' Finnegan, Belinda McKeon, Bernice Chauly, Bob Kelly, Bohdan Piasecki, Breffini Cummiskey, Brendan Hickey, Brendan Begley, Cormac Begley, Orla Barry, Buddy Wakefield, Buzz O'Neill, Carl Daly, Carl Plover, Carlos Andrés Gomez, Claire Cunningham, Danny Sheehy (Domhnall Mac Síthigh), Chris Redmond, Christy Moore, Cian O'Brien, Ciara Ní É, Clare Flynn, Claire Leadbitter, Iseult Byrne, Claus Hebor, Connor O'Brien (Villagers), Colm Mac Con Iomaire, Colm Ó Foghlú, Colm Ó Snodaigh, Colm Keegan, Cormac Begley, David Keegan, Damien Dempsey, Dani Gill, Darragh Doyle, Dara Yeats, Dave Allen, Dave Hope, Dave Tynan, David Hynes, David Keenan, David Kirker, Davin O'Dwyer, Dean Scurry, Denise Dunne, Deanna Rogers, Declan Meade, Danny Carroll, Declan O'Rourke, Deirdre Errity, Dave Judge, Derek Dodd, Dermot Bolger, Dermot Kennedy, Dil Wickremasinghe, Dominic Taylor, Don Smith, Donal Gunne, Donal Ryan, Donal O'Kelly, Donal Dineen, Donal Scannell, Dwayne Woods, Dylan Cobourn Gray, Siobhan Kane, Eddie Keegan, Edel Doran, Edel Moss, Eileen Flynn, Eimear Cheasty, Eithne Ní Chatháin (Inni-K), Elaine Feeney, Elder Roche, Elizabeth Moen, Elizabeth Whyte, Emma Connors, Emmet Condon, Emmet Kirwan, Enda Reilly, Erica Flemming, Felicia Olusanya, Fiach Moriarty, Fiachra Gaffney, Finn Keanan, Finbar Furry, Frank Phelan, Gary Dunne, Gary Gannon, Gary Sheehan, Gemma Tipton, Geoff Finan, Gerry McNamara, Gerry Smyth, Gerry Hodgers, Glen Hansard, Grace Dyas, Grainne Clear, Graham Thew, Prof. Heather Jones, Hannah Pender, Harry Leech, Hazel Hogan, Hilary Adam White, Imelda May, Ingrid Harper, Inua Ellams, Irina Lekhmus, Jane Alger, Jamie D'Alton, Jeanne Lakatos, Jeff Ballard, Jen Coppinger, Jennifer Cullen Daly, Jennifer Matthews, Jessica Frye, Jess Kav, Jem Mitchell, Jim Culleton, Jinx Lennon, Joan Daly, Joe Keenan, Joe Woods, John Byrne, John Colbert, John Reynolds, John Glennon, John Kenyon,

John Cummins, John Moynes, John Spillane, John Sheahan, Julian Gough, JP Swaine, Kalle Ryan, Karen Walshe, Karen Spellman, Karl Parkinson, Kate Dennis, Katie Smith, Keiron Campbell Black, Kerrie O'Brien, Kerryann Conway, Kevin McGloughlin, Kevin McManamom, Kim Cunningham, Kim Haughton, Kit Fryatt, Laura Larkin, Laura McCabe, Lewis Kenny, Liam Ó Maonlaí, Linda Devlin, Linda Plover, Lisa O'Neill, Lisa Hannigan, Little John Nee, Liz Reapy, Máire Logue, Máire Dineen, Máire Saaritsa, Mairead Duffy, Marcus Lynam, Marian Fitzpatrick, Mark Flynn, Mark O'Brien, Mark O'Rowe, Mark William Jones, Martin Byrne, Martin Colthorpe, Martin Dyar, Marty Mulligan, Mary Molly, Matt Bartlett, Maureen Kennelly, Maurice Sweeney, Melissa Nolan, Mia Gallagher, Mongoose, Moray Bresnihan, Morgan O'Reilly, Molly Sterling, Muireann Ní Chonnaill, Myles O'Reilly, Natasha Purtill, Nialler9, Niall James Holohan, Niamh Ní Chonchubhair, Nicole Eve Rourke, Noel O'Grady, Nollaigh Healy, Nora Hickey, Nuala O'Neill, Olga Barry, Orla Sweeney, Ollie Burns, Pat Ingoldsby, Pat Kinevane, Pat Boran, Patricia Fitzgerald, Paul Curran, Paul Casey, Paul Noonan (Bell X1), Paula Meehan, Penny Hart, Pearse McGloughlin, Philip King, Phil Lynch, Raven, Rachel Breslin, Ray Beggans, Ray Heffernan, Ray Yeats, Rhob Cunningham, Roddy Doyle, Rónán Ó Snodaigh, Ro Byrne, Robert Horsfall, Roger Gregg, Robbie Walsh, Rosita Wolfe, Ross Killeen, Ross Breen, Rowena Neville, Ruairí McKiernan, Sally Foran, Sandra James, Sarah Clancy, Sarah Balen, Sarah Maria Griffin, Sarah Brennan, Sarah Ryder, Sheena Madden, Sarah Jackson, Sarah Webb, Saint Sister, Sean Lyons, Sean Rocks, Seamus Fogarty, Selina Guinness, Shane Sutton, Simon Daniels, Simon Daniels, Siobhan Kane, Sorcha Fox, Stephen Clare, Stephen Kennedy, Stephen Murray, Stephen Murphy, Steven Camden (Polarbear), Steve Simpson, Suzanne Doyle, Tara Harrison, Tiffany Choong, Tom Donegan, Tony Clayton-Lea, Tony Walsh, Tina Robinson, Uná Molly, Ye Vagabonds, Vanessa Fox O'Loughlin, Wallis Bird, Wissame Cherfi, Wojtek Cichon, Zlata Filipovic. SORRY IF I LEFT YOU OUT!

Organisations: Arlen House, Dublin UNESCO City of Literature, Poetry Ireland, City2Cities Holland, Geen Daden Maar Woorden Festival Rotterdam, The Barbican London, Writing on the Wall

Liverpool, Frankfurt Poetry Slam, Centre Culturel Irlandais Paris, Vilenica International Literary Festival Slovenia, AVIVA, TVS's The Six O'Clock Show & Ireland AM, RTÉ's Today Show, VerseFest Canada, Spoke & Bird Singapore, Electric Picnic, Indiependance Festival, A Playful City, Seven Towers, Milk & Cookies, Scene of the Rhyme, VoiceBank, DeBarra's, Poets Anonymous, Rite & Recite, Axis Ballymum, Mermaid Arts Centre Bray, The Workmans, James Joyce Centre, Bloomsday Festival, Phiz Fest, Knockanstockan, Warriors of the Light, Kenny's Bar Lahinch, Born Optimistic, Fishamble, Munster Literary Centre, Homebeat, Hotpress, Flatlakes Festival, Fighting Words, Another Love Story, Young Hearts Run Free, Near FM, South Dublin Libraries, Body & Soul, Dublin Fringe Festival, Irish Embassy London, The Monday Echo, Slam Sunday, Flying South, First Fortnight, Nighthawks, The Brownbread Mixtape, The Co Club, Lingo Festival, ILFD, Midnight Mango, Sound Advice, Jawdropper, O'Bheal, Cúirt, First Fortnight, Cáca Milis Cabaret, Irish Writers Centre, The People Speak, Culture Vultures, Other Voices, National Concert Hall, St. Patricks Festival, Dublin Cuture Connects, National Gallery of Ireland, The Abbey Theatre, Glastonbury Festival, RTÉ Arena, RTÉ Poetry Show, Grace Photography, IADT, The Zodiac Sessions, Design for Life, Georgetown Literary Festival, Malaysia, Bewley's Café Theatre, The Civic Theatre Tallaght, Ireland Week LA, The Oscar Wilde Awards, Literary Death Match, London Irish Centre Camden, The Back Loft, Arbutus Yarns, Listowel Writers' Week, This Ain't No Disco, Nuyorican Poetry Café NYC, The Winding Stairs, Garter Lane, Waterford Youth Arts, Cill Rialaig, Crescent Arts Centre Belfast, The Whitehouse Poets Limerick, On The Nail, Stanzas Festival, Songs in the Key of D, Tongue Fu, The Lazy Band, Arthurs Bar, The International Bar, Wicklow Street, The Project Arts Centre, Reic, Whelans, Abner Browns.

Stephen James Smith is a Dublin poet and playwright central to the rise of the vibrant spoken word genre in Ireland today. In 2014 he co-founded LINGO Festival, Ireland's only spoken word festival, and is poetry curator of the annual First Fortnight Festival. The video for his poem *Dublin You Are,* which was commissioned by Dublin City Council, went viral receiving 250,000 views in 3 days. His ABSOLUTE Dublin Fringe play *Three Men Talking About Things They Kinda Know About* (2011), co-written with Colm Keegan and Kalle Ryan, was shortlisted for the Bewley's Little Gem Award. *Arise and Go!,* his debut album with musician Enda Reilly, was selected by *Hot Press* as one of the best albums of 2011. He won the Cúirt International Literary Festival Poetry Grand Slam in 2010. Stephen founded The Glór Sessions in 2009. This weekly poetry and music event ran for three years and is considered instrumental in establishing Ireland's spoken word movement.

Stephen has performed at many Irish festivals, including the Dublin Writers' Festival, Cúirt International Festival of Literature, Electric Picnic, Dublin Fringe Festival, Festival of World Cultures and Spirit of Folk; and across the globe in New York, Chicago, Iowa City, Montreal, Ottawa, Paris, Glastonbury, Amsterdam, Frankfurt, Utrecht, Ljubljana and Warsaw. He was invited to perform for the Irish Olympic team in London 2012. His work has been translated into Irish, Spanish, Slovenian, Polish, Dutch and Italian. His poetry videos have also been screened at film festivals at home and abroad, and he has featured in programmes and documentaries for television such as RTÉ's IFTA-award-winning documentary *WB Yeats: No Country for Old Men; The Works* (RTÉ); *News Today* (RTÉ); and *Like a Virgin* (RTÉ). Stephen's poetry is included on the syllabus at Western Connecticut State University and he conducts poetry workshops in secondary schools around Ireland.

www.StephenJamesSmith.com

@SJSwords

For bookings contact Matt Bartlett at www.midnightmango.co.uk